emdash

& ellipses

a chapbook
by Tanzila Ahmed

ISBN-13: 978-1523287383
ISBN-10: 1523287381

for my people

Table of Contents

Poems to Scream

Collidescope[1]

I want to spray paint drones with a stenciled *keffiyeh* print
And *henna* pattern handguns
And pixelate grenades
And calligraphy *"Bismillah"* onto bullets.

I want to tile rainbow Skittles onto black hoodies
And tattoo *hijabi* pin-up girls
And tie-dye a twisted turban
And sew old prayer rugs into superhero capes.

And when that shit explodes
It will be like glass bangles glitter bombing the world -
Life will whip through our *mehndi* stained hair
As if we are ride-or-dying fast on skateboards spangled with *desi*
truck art,
Bull's-eyes will be circled in the rings of light around the new
moon,
Pastel colored chalk outlines on the ground will be abundant and
in the shape of faded shadows.

This world
So imploded
Blood stained *chadors* will be used as white flags
Of surrender no more.

---

[1] Published in *I Am A Warrior* Oakland Asian Cultural Center's Second Zine, Fall 2015

Cut From the Same Cloth[2]

Threading through my veins
Your being needles into my soul
Two sides of the world
Seamed into one.
It was your calloused fingers
That caressed the cloth now on my bare skin -
It was your brow sweat
That soaked into these stitches -
It was your tired hot breath
That weaves into this stretch.

We were cut from the same cloth
- You and I -
Patterned from the same likeness,
Our brown skin coating us
Like *amarah bhoan*
Distant cousins
Ripped apart at the motherland.
Except,
This one here was destined for economic export
And you were destined to industry at home.

My land of opportunity
Is quilted with your life.
In this global economy
Bangladesh is tattooed into the fabric of America.
Yet xenophobia frays at our existence here
Othered into being from there.
Unwelcomed by those who wear these clothes.
My label may be threadbare and faded
But make no mistake

---

[2] Recorded as an audio track for *Beats for Bangladesh Benefit Album*, June 2014

The tag on the back of my neck reads
"Made In Bangladesh" too.
I am kind of like you-

Where your last touch
Destined for America
Is my first touch
Longing for home-
Where the *whirrrrr*
Of your Singer machine
Is my Tagore song
Tugging me for more -
Where your
Survival tenacity
Makes me unravel
To the core.

It is your warm blood
That seeps into the seams
Of the rubbled factory floor.
It is your singed skin
That is stitched
Into these conflicted clothes.
It is your salted tears
Squeezing out
Of the needle eye.
With just a switch of a stitch
How simple your life mine could have been.

We are cut from the same cloth,
You and I.
I may not be Bangladeshi -
But I am "Made in Bangladesh"
Too.
Two sides of the world
Seamed into one.

Look at them.

They are protecting him.

Where was Usaama Rahim's manhunt where he was caught alive and uninjured?

...surrounded and shot while at a bus stop.

Where was Mike Brown's state sanctioned bulletproof vest?

...as he raised his hands up.

Where was Eric Garner's excuse of "mental illness"?

...while suffocated with a choke hold.

Where was Oscar Grant's freedom to not be handcuffed?

...as he got shot in the back.

Where was Freddie Gray's infantilizing shirt tug on the way to the backseat of the air condition police car?

...found dead in the back of a police van.

When does 12 yr. old Tamir Rice get to be "just a kid"?

...as he played with a toy gun in the park.

Look.

Look at how they are protecting him.

How About It...Now[3]

The President's Post Racial America
Appeals to me
I would like to see this fantastical myth
Come to be
If you believe
In "hope" and "change" too
Then share 'em with me
Don't keep 'em all for you.

Show me that you mean
Democracy, please -
Cause from parking lots of Chapel Hill to streets of Ferguson,
Gurdwaras in Oak Creek to an AME church in Charleston,
From the hands of police in Baltimore to the hands of police in
Alabama's Madison,
I'm beat to my knees.

You can't fund the Arab Spring and the Umbrella Revolution,
Shoot Mike Brown and Trayvon Martin,
Freddie Gray and Tamir Rice,
Ezell Ford and Rekia Boyd,
Then make fine speeches
About Freedom's "Forward" Way.

Looks like by now
You ought to know
There's no chance to beat Global Apartheid
By protecting the NEW Jim Crow.
Freedom's not just
To be won Over There
It means Freedom at home, too
Now – right here.

---

[3] Poetry Remix of *How About It* by Langston Hughes, 1942

Pass me the mic
I need to amplify the margins.
Give me some ink
The stories of "others" need to be told.
Bless me with words
Suffocated histories need to be heard
Legacy has been blurred
Stifled and tortured.
Words.
Words need to explode.

Blast my fingertips with inspiration
Because it's with desperation
A ferocity of purpose
That claws at my voice box
Scratches in my paper
Grits my tongue-tip
Rips me with rapture.
Because it's not my words
But rather yours-
Your words
I want heard.

Tell me.
Tell me your story.
Your story is my history,
Your story makes me, me.
Your words are my words.
Combined legacy.

Where your transnational built my identity.
Where your intifada is my mutiny.
Where your blood made my society.

Where your 1984 is my 9/11.
Where your partition is my immigration.
Your concentration is my colonization.

Where your Selma let me vote.
Where my plane is your boat.
Where borders crossed you
And people crossed me.
Where my rights were your wrongs,
My fights your dreams,
My light your reality.

Words like gumdrops dance in my head
With messages to be said
Waiting to be bled.

This.
This is where
The act of storytelling is injustice fighting.
Poetry fiending - annihilating.
Writing is rioting.
Lyrics enlightening.
My soul craves to unbury the dead
Give life to the struggles that went unsaid.

Like a seed of a weed
Piercing pavement cracks,
Stretching for sun rays
And gutter drops to snatch -
I too crave to break,
Break for thirst,
Thirst to breathe,
Breathe to live.
Fight to survive.
My words cannot be concreted.

Your words -
I can't let be concreted.

Give me breath -
From lips to fingertips to lyrics,
Stencil to spray paint to markers,
Bullhorn to wheat paste to posters.

Give me space -
From stage to walls to concrete overpass,
From sky to paper to stenciled glass
Skin to twitter to manicured grass.

Give me breath.
Give me space.
Give me anything
So I can say something.

Pass me the mic.
I need to amplify the margins.
I have words
Words that need to explode.

To build
We must
Dig into the cracks
Unbury the truth
Life seeping into concrete
Invisible blood, running just underneath
Superficially tell the stories
These clean streets
Of Ferguson can never be bleached
My peoples DNA permanently
Embedded in dirt roads of partition
The stench of injustice
Just under the pavement of Fruitvale Station
Train tracks of Ahmedabad
Derailed on terror striations
Rana Plaza, Gaza, LA, and Brooklyn
Hong Kong, Bellingham, Selma, and Oakland

Our skin is soiled
So we must scratch
Digging into the brown
Until the dirt under our nails
Tell the stories defiantly
Finger painting sunlit skies
With mud blood ink
Fists brush the clouds
Reaching out for stars
voice // water// breath
For a hand to clasp down from the sky
Fingers twinkling not to be saved
- Oh no -
These hands are reaching to survive
They are digging for life

To build
We must excavate our hearts
Till the light shines divine
Our struggle is our shovel
And love is our guiding light
Imagine what we could do
If you let me truly love you
The glasshouse sheltering our fragile hearts
Would come tumbling down
Rebuilt with mud huts of legacy and bravery
With fingerprints of vulnerability
With clay rawness mending gaps
With soft touches that listen
With our hands
Together we can build sandcastles to the sky
Till the stars reach back
And we would finally inhale light
Exhale love
And our blood would pour on the streets no more...
Now. How radical is that?

The little girl cries // Her mother hides her in fear
The military comes knocking // In the closet they're cloaked in
Allah & tears
The older boys run // Through the rice filed to the nation's border
Bottle rocket, shots ring out // Life is chaotic disorder
With fists in the air // Students mob curfew-ed streets
Fighting for freedom, they voice// Dissent, fight, rinse and
repeat...

This isn't one story but the story of many
The hidden history belonging to you and me.
This is the story of IDP Tamil refugees
Bangla speaking farming revolutionaries
Burmese monks with bowls down for freedom to pray
Flotillas to Gaza floating through inhumane blockade
Oscar Grant executed in the back by an Oakland cop
Ayana Jones, Sean Bell, Mike Brown - the police killings never
stop.

Curfews, bullets, blood soaked pavement
Dictators, military regime, civilian dissident
Protest signs, censorship, wartime prisoners
Secret meetings, refugees, no housing – just hunger...

Awaz karo // For all the girls and boys.
Make noise // For the entire world to hear.
The histories of the past //How they try to make us forget
Our stories pushed to the margins// But we must always
remember our footsteps.
They struggle for freedom //But it's our struggle too.
Remember and organize //Revolution anew....

Make noise for the freedom fighters taking it to the streets.
Make noise for the people with revolution as heartbeats.

Awaz karo - make noise - with all our voices united
No justice, no peace
Together we cannot be defeated.

I have lost my origin story.
She is buried six feet under America's soil
Wrapped in white
No nation-state can define her now
And I no longer remember
For whom/what/why I was fighting for.

I had asked her once –
"How do you say *vote* in Bangla?"
My mother's tongue paused and replied with –
"VOTE"
Thickly, adding H's after consonants and rounding vowels long
As Bengalis were known to do
So that I double-taked
Almost believing her words were authentically Bangla
Before realizing
I had been tricked and I guess, so had she.
How would she have known?
Democracy had always chased her, escaped her
The Bangla word for voting as foreign to her
As it was to me.

1947 – Partition drove my Nana out from Calcutta in the newly
formed India
Into Dhaka of the newly formed East Pakistan.
1956 – In the midst of the Bengali Language Movement
Where language rebels of East Pakistan fought
Against the Urdu dominant oppressors,
My mother was born.
Her birth certificate an eyewitness testimony
Of her coming to life.

---

[4] Commissioned by PolicyLink for Equity Summit, 2015

1971 – As a teen, she escaped Lahore, Pakistan
With the clothes on her back on the first flight back to Dhaka
Eventually trading in her Pakistani passport
For one from the newly minted nation of Bangladesh.
1978 – Her Bangladeshi passport was stamped
With an American spouse visa for the husband she hardly knew,
And carrying me in her belly -
An anchor baby along for the ride.
Nov 21st, 1986 – I waved an American flag
As she recited the pledge of allegiance at the ceremony,
My mother holding in her hand her certificate of naturalization.
A citizen of a nation state she had finally become.
1988 - I went with her to the polls
As she voted for the first time, possibly ever.
1998 – She took the 18-year-old version of me
Her first eligible offspring
To the polls to vote for the time, ever.
2011 – Her death certificate
Under the 'race' category listed "Asian, Muslim"
Which – given her history – seemed appropriately misappropriated
somehow.
Her transnational identity was uncategorizable.

I keep her stack of documents safe, still.
As if they still mean something -
Passports from three countries,
Birth, immigration, naturalization and death certificates -
In these papers are her roots of uprooted civic belonging.

To vote means to have ownership of a *home*
But did she know the legacy that she swore into?
The battles that were fought here, too?
1923's Bhagat Singh Thind's Supreme Court case
1946's Luce Cellar Act
1964's Civil Rights Act
1965's Immigration Act

1965's Voting Rights Act – and of course -
The 2001's Patriot Act
The one that undid them all...
The one that made her perpetually a second-class citizen...

Where does one even belong?
When moving borders hold the power to define
And citizenship evades transnational trans-historical identities?
In this second-class reality, where is your ability to be?

I have lost my origin story.
And it is her I am fighting for.

It's not your fault, you know.
These streets were never paved with gold
They were made to control impossible dreams
Not the marginalized immigrant reality.

You tried, I can see.
As an economic refugee of the 1970s,
You were the first of now 5,000 Angelino-Bangladeshis
With a degree in engineering you are
One of only 45% of Bangladeshis to get a Bachelors degree
You bought your own house and your own car in your twenties
You brought over your bride-to-be then
You had me.
It was the 1980s immigrant American dream.

It was systematic, understand?
Internalized bias and racism led to a constant job search
For that perfect work culture fit.
Long-term employment affects Asian Americans
disproportionately -
You were simply surviving
And quickly learned that minimum wage was not actually living
That blue collared life would lead
To a lifetime of struggle
To access equitable healthcare, education
Or fresh food and fresh air.

It was structural, not individual, get it?
Because data showed that people of color under a certain per capita
Were not meant to access these.

---

[5] Commissioned by PolicyLink for Equity Summit, 2015

In our family healthcare was needed
Because the home you could afford was right next to the freeway
Because children who live near freeways have a higher risk of
chronic asthma
Because Asian American girls have a higher rate of depression and
suicide
Because as aging South Asians, you and Mom collectively
Battled high blood pressure, high cholesterol, diabetes.
That your wife would die from complications with her obesity
And that 34% of South Asians die from heart disease.
Because all this data tells us, is factual racial hierarchy.

But you didn't know, you were a pawn in this data disparity.
Law enforcement is racial profiling
FBI is surveilling
Islamophobes are hate-criming
Sallie Mae is education debt collecting
Workplaces are discriminating and firing.

You are proud, I know.
But it's not you.
It is class, race, migrant and language -
These systems othered you into the margins of
Environmental, employment, healthcare, and education equity.
Discrimination,
Disparity,
Disproportionately,
Inequality.
Systematic supremacy.

But how were you to know, really?
They kept calling you a model minority.
And with no data to prove it.

Khothay Aasha?
Faded. Berated.
Inspiration mis-communicated.
Running. Seeking.
Like a mad woman breaking.
Lost at all cost.
Hope seems to have been tossed.

Aashou Aasha.
Come, let us rediscover
Like long lost lovers.
Come, let me cradle you in my arms
Smother you in warmth
Water you with desire
Find and grow in you what I missed.

Aasha.
Hope.
Come; let me find hope again
For the people in the 9th ward
For the people whose life is one cheek swab away
For the people where suicide seems like the only option
For the girls in South Asia where corruption keeps literacy at bay.

Let me find hope
For the people going to bed hungry every night
For the forests being stripped of life
For Mother Nature's poisoning
For the domestically abused women
For the homeless
For the poverty stricken.

Let me find hope

For the youth with their whole life ahead of them
For the elderly looking back on the life they are leaving behind
Let me find hope
Because even though we live In a system too big to change...
I need to find hope that oppression can be defeated
Justice can be had for all
Systems can have radical revolution.

Aamer Aasha.
My hope.
You were never lost.
I simply didn't know where to look.
You were within all along.

Ice Cream Truck

The sound of carnival organs
Playing a metallic Yankee Doodle Dandee
From the neon emblazoned creeping truck
Invokes a nostalgic reaction
From my longing belly
'Slow Children' it says but
The missing comma says everything,
As the Brown-Hyphen-American neighbor-kids
Chase hot pavement
Empty-handed bare-footed.
Americana iconic
The ice cream trucks circling this hood
Always carry Mexican Vero mango chili suckers
And Lucas lime dust
And the drivers never speak in English.
A long shadowed hot afternoon
After a day of summer fasting
My belly grumbles as the organ sounds
Incite memories of melting Popsicle juices
Sugar highs and brain freezes
And I crave cold nostalgic flavors
Combined with hot iftar satiations.
In delirious hunger, I wonder if
Push-pops and ice cream cones
Come in date flavors or Rooh Afza syrups
And why all the ice cream trucks
Disappear after the streetlights go on
After azaan calls us inside to break fast for the day.

Dhaka

The plane descends on the Dhaka tamasha
Of the rickshaw peddling rickshaw-wallahs
Crowding the narrow filthy streets
With *chohk, chohk, chohk* reds, yellows, and neon greens
Kajol-eyed painted ladies
Filmi heroes fighting gallantly on plastic canopies.

The fast and furious soup-ed up rides
Consist of horsepower
In the form of just one checkered,
Lungi-ed mustachio-ed man
Spin spin spinning the bedazzled rimmed tricycle
Laden heavy with a purda-ed family of six,
Or piled high with garments going
Straight to Wal-Marts in Missouri,
Or a slightly pudgy golden sari wrapped auntie.
Takas are thrown, seats are dusted
And the rickshaw-wallah lingers for another ride.

In old Dhaka the streets are so narrow and crowded
Cars are humbled and rickshaws reign supreme.

I grip the slick seat dramatically
Adrenaline pumping through my veins
As I search for seat belts,
Or handle bars,
Or helmets.
The only cycling I knew was stationary
And in the safety of spin class
Where my guide was a skinny blonde bitch in spandex.

Would this have been my reality?
A salwar wearing woman with the don't-fuck-wit-me swagger
A deshi girl popping pani puris street side

Riding rickshaws with a cocky confidence
And haggling prices in Bangla till they were cutthroat cheap.
Owning this city, home in these streets.

Instead, I hear them talk to each other in Bangla,
"Bideshi. Russian."
In Bangla I interrupt – "I'm not Russian. I'm American & my
parents are from here."
They don't respond.

This may be the motherland of my mother tongue,
But I'll always be grasping for home.

Heart Break Beats

Thump-thump. My heart breaks into a beat
Thump-thump. My heart beats breathing life into my lifeless limbs
Thump-thump. My heart beats softly...slowly...
Warm blood melting the ice around it

Thump-thump.
My heart bleeds feelings from fingertips to feet
With every resounding beat my thoughts get louder
My nerves quiver, my blood gets warmer

Thump-thump. Thump-thump. Thump-thump.
My heart has awakened life into the loveless
The beat of my heart has awakened me to my core
Breathing heat into my soul

THUMPTHUMPTHUMPTHUMP
It beats hard, it beats fast
My heartbeats so hard so fast so fierce
Implosion feels imminent

Pumping blood rushes through my veins
Nerves race energy at lightning speed
Muscles burn in fiery sensations
My heart beats ablaze

I feel every vibration every touch is magnified
The wind from a butterfly
The touch of an angel
The kiss of life
I feel everything

Every feeling expounded, sensation exploded
Emotions inside me burst with unbelievable intensity
Everything feels everything.

———

Pain. Joy. Sorrow. Compassion. Grief. Passion. Happiness.
Sadness. Hate.
And love.
Oh, love.

My heart forgot what love felt like but I feel love again.
My heart beats love fiercely pumping through my veins.

THUMPTHUMPTHUMPTHUMP
Implosively my heart beat
Thunderously painfully overwhelmingly
I cry. I want. I hate. I laugh. I need. I see. I blind. I love. I feel. I
break. I heal.
I beat. My heart. It beats.
Thump – thump. It beats. For him.

My heart breaks into a beat that breathes life into the loveless.
I'm reminded that a heart beating without love
Is lifeless.

Falling at the Grand Canyon

I look up and kiss the sky,
Blue with hazy gray.
At this cliff I am in it
Practically touching sun's rays.

I peer down over the edge
Crevice into the center of the earth.
At this bluff I am in it
Practically falling into her embrace.

Shadow play on pink strata
Sunset paint brushing mountainsides.
It's hard not to believe in Allah
When this feels like a forehead kiss from Allah.

My fear of falling is in full effect.
Glances down put my heart in my throat.
It makes my tummy flip in that flip flopping way
Where I think I've found the guy to love...

Which leads me to believe that wasn't love I felt.
Just a fear of falling.
Or maybe love and fear and fear and love,
Are one and the same.

You need a little bit of both.
Maybe I just need to stand
At the canyon's edge
Letting all inhibitions go.

Poems to Whisper

Theory

What is
The theory of change
To radical love,
To love radically?

Respectability

The interviewer asked
As you get older
Do you ever get tired
Of being polite?

How To Sleep

I
Dream
In
Poetry
And
Rage.

Make It Real

How do we harness
Our own power
To manifest?
How do we
Re-imagine our truth?

But where
Does that leave
This stifled split tongue of
American idioms and
Migrant colloquialism?
A speak pattering
Pidgin on tangled lips
Stuttering to staccato
A lisp that
Straddles borders with a
Cadence of hyphenation -
Not quite voiceless
But voices less.

Bholo

You make me yearn for my mother tongue.
My brown fingers intertwine yours as I pull you – *eedhigay* -
towards me
Lips graze your neck – *asthay* - as my instincts form soft sounds
Saved only for special people.
"Choloh," I whisper in your ear as I tug you into the dark.

My words are incomplete
Grasping at breath for a language that sits with me unfinished.
Mother tongue is no longer fully my own,
Hyphenated into perpetuity,
Taken to the grave.
I speak at grade school level and my pronunciation
Is halfway around the world.
This language is frustrated
Driven to the surface when angry - and I guess -
When I'm in love.
Implicitly my mouth aches to create a language of home with you.
A common language of love.
A taste of us.

When you are near
I'm surprised at how this tongue rises to lick sweet nothings into
your ears.
It is distantly yours as well
And clumsily our ancestral muscle memories
Seek remembrance in expressions of which was once ours.
Into you I fold.
You kiss me like it's your birthright.
My being has turned instinctive. Guttural. Reactionary.
Your arms slink slowly around my back
Wordsmithing what your throat catches.
Our brown skin merging into one translation.

A vocabulary incomplete,
Touch lilts what struggling voices cannot.
Aasho - your skin tastes.
Eekhanay - my fingers trace.
Aanando - your palm caresses.
Aaro. More. *Aakhon*. Right now.
Amar praan. My soul.
In you, my words find home.

B-Side Girl

When you write about me, tell the world how
I almost loved you. And how beautiful it
almost could have been. Use exotic allegories
without being oriental and a cadence of a
heart skipping a beat. Fill the ellipses between us
with desert symbolisms and roaming distances. Put to lyrics
the emdash of an open water almost kiss. Insert
a haunting hook that never leaves pressed lips. Make it
an A-side-third-single track that makes listeners wonder
why you could never love a girl like that back. Write
about me like a dream you never want to forget.

And then play it – till you never want to listen to it again.

Foreign Language

You never learned to say
"I love you," did you?
In your mother tongue
The way that lovers do.
My patois renders me colonized
Your pidgin falls on me foreign
Our tongues pull at love clumsily
Leaving a tear soaked trail
From the language of home.
Let's speak like we were meant
Where love and home intersect
And the language of love
Is muted no more.
Let's love tongue-tied
Decolonized
Till it feels like home.

Oxytocin

Touch me to remind me that my skin
Breathes life and that my living
Is not in solitude. Remember
How my blood is warm,
Electrified by your graze. My
Heart beats with your caress.
I had forgotten. Your touch.
How I craved it. How it
Reminded me to be alive.
I am life.
Touch me.
I want to live,
Once more.

Love In The Time of Surveillance

I often wonder
Of all of my ex-lovers
Which one was a spy.

Melancholic Love

It's the sadness in love at first sight.
The melancholy of a knee melting first kiss
The loneliness with a cheek resting on his warm chest
The missing when tenderly cuddled in his arms.

It's the longing for his touch when holding hands
The fear of quivering inner thighs
The bitterness in tasting his sweetness on lips
The grief while screaming in ecstasy.

The falling in this moment
Is but already a passing memory
I want it so badly
But it was over from the start.

I feel a stir behind me,
Naked and spooned.
My eyes flutter.
They don't need to open for me to know
The outside world is dark
And a street light shines a ray inside.

The rest of me is perfectly still, waiting.
Anticipating.
His breath at the nape of my neck -
in and out, in and out -
Steady, deeply asleep.
Though, I can tell, not quite completely.

I shift slight -
My nakedness pulls along his length
So that I sink deeper into his warm fold.
In his arms
I want to be seen.
The invisible burka of bravado
Disintegrates.
In his bed
There's no fear of arousal.

In the dark outside world
Chills run through my veins daily
As my skin shrouds me in constant questions.
Daggering gazes paint targets on my Brownness,
As my eyes avoid contact.
I try to fly under the radar of drones
Where no means no means stop and frisk
My body is policed by other's fears
And my agency belongs to the NSA.

To avoid arousing suspicion
I fold into myself
Suspicious of Freedom
And Liberty for Everyone.
In god we trust, only
And only in me.

But here,
In his bed
In the holding cells of his arms,
I feel his lips on my neck kiss.
Here, I want to be craved for my Brown skin
His tongue licks at my fears
He searches into the depths of my Brown eyes
His fingers slowly frisk my body seeking more
He's awoken,
Pulling me deeply.
Completely.

In his arousal
Is the only place I want to be seen.

Safe to Dream

Sometimes I dream so hard
That the line between
What is real and otherworldly blurs.

I travel to lands,
Fly through space,
Float on oceans
In constant motion in my sleep
Untethered when awake
I pretended like they were nothing,
Trying hard to forget
Too frightened to lose my place
Too easily getting lost to dreams.

"What did you dream?" you'd whisper in my neck.
In your arms with my eyes closed
I felt safe to remember how to dream again.
So I told you about
The tumultuous waters,
The moving colors,
The visitors from other lands.
Tethered by your embrace,
You believed in my magic
So I could believe, too.

How Do You Love

I ask
Instead
"Did you dream last night?"
If this world is but a dream
I wonder
Instead
What is your version of reality.
How in the other world did you see?
Did you love or fly?
Did you visit past lives?
Did our minds collide
Behind your sleeping eyes?
Did you dance through metaphors?
Did you write in poetic Technicolor?
Was it the adventure
Where you finally talked to her?
You say,
Instead,
"I don't remember."
I wonder
Instead
What is your version of dreams.
How in this world can you see...

First Kiss

Remember how they said
First kisses were like fireworks?
Like explosions in the sky
Could be thrilled in two lips.
Kind of...
Maybe.

A fistful of matches
A pyromaniac at heart
Chasing the glowing sparklers' reign of fire
Squeeeeeeeeeee- BOOM!
When the smoke clears
All that's left
Are the charred remains of the firecracker shells
And the taste of singed skies
Kind of...
Maybe.

Falling For You

There is
Lust
And
Love
But what is it
When you just want
To be touched?
When a kind caress
Is all you crave?

Careful Dance

You used to almost love me.
Your thumb grazed my lip
For that almost kiss
Just a look could render you speechless
"I'm trying hard not to fall in love with you,"
You had said.
But what I heard was
You used to almost love me.
We were always a mess of longing.

Vertigo

The green vertigo
turned crimson violet in the
cipher of his lips.

I Have No Words

Surprised, tongue-tied
I'm rendered speechless
By fingertip kisses
Speaking silent words in poetic caresses.

The indents leave imprints
Of sweet torment,
Touch runs deep silencing me
Inking my soul with legacy.

Metaphors escape as liquid my limbs do turn.
Similes evade like a lover's after burn.
Alliteration alludes all away
Meter of heart beats skips into disarray.
In-articulation.
Has no rhyme or reason.

"Read," he says.
Write, I say.
Stroke me with your words,
And I'll be your paper.

He hovered above me
His hand slowly running down
Against my bare chest.
It paused
Skin on skin
Hand to heart,
Sunrays piercing through the
Nooks and crannies created
In the space between
Hugs,
Touch,
Embrace.
"I've never been
with anyone who was
the same color as me," he whispered
in his soft and sexy way.
"That is problematic," I sighed slowly.
I looked at his fingers on my chest
Skin tone blending into one
Slowly shifting
Skin on skin
Brown sugar hands
stirring in chai colored magic.
Surprising at how tones can blend so effortlessly
With legacies of differences
Yet a perfect palette match.
Skin on skin
Brown on brown
Blended into one.
We spun around
Brown in brown
Till one.

Hands grasp wrists above head.
Eyes lock. I look away.
Teeth flit at hip skin.
Lips grasp. I flinch twist.
Firm bites at nipple tips.
Sigh rips. I resist.
Licks flick shoulder blades
Nails trail spine
Tongue traces path from taunt neck
To tender breasts to pulsation.

I pull back till I can no more.
Futile to seduction I release
Succumbing to his lips, touch, tongue,
Gaze, breath, press, weight, motion, mold,
His soul centered in me.

I quiver vulnerably, a box unlocked.
Something's been opened.
"You're trembling."
I nod, head sinking further in pillow.
He sinks further in me till the shakes come so fast
Trembles buzz humming to euphoric bliss.

And all I see is green vertigo
Taste sweat
Feel joy/grief/compassion/aggression/tears
All emotions all at once.

I bite
Pushed beyond the brink of ecstasy
Beyond the point of no return
Beyond where I belong to me.
I am now his.

I lay raw cradled in his arms
His finger tracing sweat along the seam of naked body.
Kisses peppered. Skin to skin with lover.

"This is what a lover should be. To be here. Like this.
To learn your body completely.
To adore you the way you deserve to be."

My tummy flips, heart beat trips
Tongue is tied with naked shy.
"There are so many things I want to do to you..."
He whispers in my ear,
Hair grasped, pulled back.
Breath gasps.

"All in good time," I whisper rough
As I let him draw me under folding into his deep embrace
As my soul opens up to another raw sexual danger.

Lover without love.
Making love with a stranger.
Vulnerable with a lover.

Regretful Tease

I taste your scent like sweet regret
Tongue laced with sweat, rain, and skin.
Lips swollen like an invitation.

Images of water kissed foggy car windows
Sensations of soft spine-tingling breathe-taking lips
Aggressive aches from nails on skin,
Fingers in hair, teeth on neck.
Wet night air on bare skin.

My car veers on slick pavement
And I straighten, alone.
Lost in sensation and sudden loss.

I bite my puckered lips tasting your residuals,
And I wonder with unease if this is just the beginning
Or simply the end of something fleeting...

Word/Fore Play

Firm grasp - mold like clay.
Whispered words - submit to melt.
Take me. I am yours.

O

Let me submit to
Find that spot I thought I'd lost.
Explore and explode.

Devil's Play

Like the devil, he tempts
Flames lick at my soul
Persuading with lust
And the loss of control.

Tantalizing my taste
My embers he still holds,
Left wondering if this emptiness
His lips can still console.

We

Behind closed eyes
We paint pink bursts
Pulsing aqua threads
Gold bling ecstasy

The soft punk
With a sterling heart
Has fierce love.
Hard core is full of melting fire,
Tender sex is brimmed with grit,
And passion is raw.

Icy lust and plush love
Crash together into a punk-drunk romance
Leaving broken ice pieces
Scattered
Rebelliously melting softly
Into pulling you under.

A heart that is raw-ly grit
A soul that is gritting-ly raw
Is the soft love
Of a hard core.

Firm arms, bulging biceps
Embrace me as I awaken.
Warm breath on neck
Provides a virtual blanket.

I'm upset
From last night's fight.
I want to cuddle deep
And escape embrace
Both at the same time.

His grip is warm and tight
Try as I might to squirm from his grasp.
"Let me go," I whisper
Back into his sleeping chest.
"Why," he firmly states
Surprisingly not heavy with sleep
Yet eyes still closed.
Holding me tighter.
His forearms intertwined across my chest
His bicep doubling as a pillow.

"Let me go," I whisper again,
Wiggling in his hold.
He's strong,
Stronger than any guy I've been with.
"Why," he states, again.
His muscles flex
Holding me closer.

I couldn't think of a reason.
I was exhausted
And emotionally taxed.
He holds

I remain quiet
And cuddle into his chest deeper.
I was tired of fighting him and my angry heart.
I just needed to be held
Firmly squeezed
Till I could resist no more.
Till I can resist no more.

Love Hungry

Writing about love when you are hungry
Makes you hungry for love
Like the bitter gourd's sweet nectar
"What makes you wake each morning," she asked
"What love propels you?"
I struggle each morning to be drawn out from my dreams
The love in them more tangible than this reality
The chasing of echoes down corridors
When all I crave is the oxytocin rush from his touch, again
And suffer withdrawals from dopamine cuddles, instead
I'm starving for skin sparks
Hungry for sleep
And with a hunger – maybe - for more.

Nature's Lip Gloss

Swollen puckered lips
After they've been freshly kissed
Plush with sensations.

Daring

Still taste him on my
lips./ He kissed till soul shook with
remember./Fucker.

Inked

"Your God is faded…"
I whispered into the poet's shoulder
Touching the faded 'Old English'
Dios.

Sticking

He told me to write about him
Narcissist.
Told him I wouldn't.
My words, I said, they are stuck.
I'm stuck.
He kissed me till my words
They became unglued.
And, inevitably, I do.

Dhuniya

The streetlight seeped in through curtain cracks dimly lighting the midnight room. My cold naked back turned towards yours. Asleep, you turn. Your forefingers flat, slowly and softly moves down my back along my spine, from neck to waist, steady as if my bone was your braille and you were reading a map, seeking a guide. I woke gently, careful not to stir, struck by the intimacy of the touch.

We loved each other as only writers could love – with ferocious silent word play where our fingertips wrote our stories into each other. Your touch was my erotica, your whispers my dhuniya.

At the small of my back your hand stops, the familiar spot where few have owned like you. Fingers stopped seeking, it had been found. Your fingers slowly wrap around to my tummy, firm forearm gliding against my naked waist. You pull me in close, till every inch is skin to skin, till your warmth stretches the length of my body. I lean into your touch, fold into being held, feeling whole, surrendering the longing and feeling complete once again. Your face nuzzles my neck sleepily, one soft kiss to my back, and your head falls back heavy on your pillow, falling quickly to satisfied sleep.
You had found what you were looking for. As had I.

A Return

Our ten-second touch
Surged oxytocin
Through our veins
Sparkling serotonin
"We both need this, don't we?" he had said.
But I guess he didn't need it enough.

Again

There is a hollowness to
      The beat of my heart
It shivers
      With each pump
Daring not to let the tears
      Cascade
Caught
      Beneath my clavicle.

I write the men in my life out of it –
As if the penning declaring yearning
Dialoguing our hearts on paper
Narrating the magic of the space in-between
Could have enveloped them into my life.

Instead,
When put to words
These men run faster than the ink dries
Unable to see themselves in prose
Unable to be read into my story.

So,
I hold back my words.
I whisper the poems to myself in my sleep
I hide away prose in the crevices of my heart
I am edited into a muted and meeker version of myself
I craft the kind of character that I think
Men are supposed to love.

Till the written word betrays me.

I thought love letters could make men fall in love with you.
They hide these notes tucked into lapels
As they pull back and drift away
Folding a corner of the page of their reality
Then fading out.
Jinxed it once again.

Put In The Work

The muted soft shell
Was not to his liking
It was too guarded, too walled, too careful.

"Be yourself," he coaxed her,
"Be vulnerable and safe with me."

Carefully he peeled away,
Asking for more than she was ready to give.
Till he held her heart in his hand.

But it was too intense, too vibrant, too real,
Too much
It was untamable.
What did he expect?
There were guards for a reason.

"Take care of yourself," he denied her.
"I don't see a romantic future between us, ever."

Don't ask for what's behind hidden walls
Unless you are prepared to hold
What has yet to be seen.

The Role of the Muse

To love,
But not to love too much.
To be adored.
But not to be confused with love.
It may be slightly under
I love you
But better than
I like to love you from afar.

Cupcakin'

I miss how he used to touch my lips
With the tip of his thumb as if they were
The buttery frosting shell on a perfect cupcake,
Lightly gliding slowly with a whisper of indentation
Anticipation
Before sinking in and pulling my mouth in for a taste.
Like it was dessert.
Something to be savored.
Kisses desired.

The organizer.
We met at a Muslim open mic where he MCed my feature.
He chased for six months till I almost loved him.
But he left me crying with an endless cipher of words.

The writer.
After a night of reading to me from books
He'd whisper seductive words into my hair as we'd fuck.
He left me breathless, wordless.
Reminding me that the words inside myself were magical too.

The poet.
He'd spit lyrics on sidewalks, under streetlights, over pillow talk
Sharing beats, dreams, and stories of revolutionaries...
His fingers stroked invisible poetry on my bare back
His tongue moved mine
Till everything spilling out of me was unbelievably lyrically.

The singer.
This Pakistani punk with the soundtrack to my identity.
He'd share his music before it was even a beat, raw and naked
Till our feelings, our bodies were raw and naked too.
In bed my finger traced the Urdu poem tattooed on his bicep,
Wondering if I could ever write poems worthy of ink to skin.

It wasn't your fault, after all.
No one warned you
Not to fall in love with a grieving girl.

No one told you the risk you were taking -
That after grief her love had no boundaries.
Her heart was an infinite abyss
Where other people's tenderness
Were rays of light cutting into it.
Such extreme darkness
Reaches balance only with
Such extreme light.
Heart wrenching turmoil and delirious happiness
Tears of pain and tears of bliss
Sobs and laughs
Taketh and receivith.

How could you have known
Your love would have been reciprocated in this way?
That she would love you like this?
That when faced with mortality
There is realization that life can end at any moment,
One loves as if life can end at any moment.
Love then, can only be recklessly,
Effortlessly and hopelessly.
It was a responsibility.
Because with a finite time on earth
And an infinite capacity to love -
That is the only way a grieving girl can love.

But you didn't know.
How could you?
She was just a time pass love in an infinite world.
You loved normal,

With hesitancy, guard, and reign.
She returned with heart on sleeve,
Unarmored and unbridled.
It was more than you could have ever asked for.
Too much more.

But that's not your fault.
How could you have possibly known?

Laughter.

I have forgotten how to laugh.

I have forgotten how to drop my guard to laugh.

I have forgotten how I sounded laughing untethered and without a care.

I have forgotten how you made me laugh, the sounds of giggles drenched past flirt.

I have forgotten how to converse through laughter, nonverbal cues streaming on top of one another.

I have forgotten how I craved to make you laugh.

I have forgotten how the sound of your laugh rippled with hesitancy, as if your hard edge façade would shatter.

I have forgotten how I could picture your crooked smile as I heard your laugh.

I have forgotten how the sound of our two laughs merged.

I have forgotten how eager you were to tease me into laughing fits.

I have forgotten how you make me want to laugh.

I have forgotten how happy these laughs made me, joy vibrating from my soul.

I have forgotten how laughs made me.

I have forgotten how you made me laugh.

I have forgotten laughs.

I have (almost) forgotten you.

Trying to Forget

It's as if my dreams
Have muscle memories of you.
Asleep my body remembers what my heart
Tried so hard to forget -
My organs still breathe in you.

Crisp Breathe

Mountain silhouettes
Glow in indigo fade to
Black to desert stars.

Light

We danced circles
On sulfer-ed streets
Under the sparkler embers
And harvest moon half shadow
To music only we
Could hear
In our heads.

Cocaine/Concrete Sunset

The intersection of the concrete madness
Of the 405, 101, 5, 710, 60, 10, 57 -
Makes sense only once.

Between day and night
Between sun and moon
When speeding through the maze
Expanse of blue gradation over sky
Twilight wind whipping your hair
Dusky glow dusting life
And cocaine sunset on the western horizon.

Only then does this madness
Seem enchanted
And this city
Full of golden possibilities -
If only for a split moment.

Tremors

I want to feel the earth shake under my feet,
The tremor of fireworks running through my vein,
The kiss of a shooting star flying by.

I want to spin till the stars overhead
Turn into a vortex sucking me in.
Dance till trembles rush folding my soul in on myself.
Fall with outstretched arms till an open embrace
Squeezes me whole.

I want to remember what it was like to have laughter spill from lips
last summer,
The pure bliss of a first kiss while standing under stars and street
lamps,
The thrill of finding an elephant while on an epic adventure for
purpose.

Earthquake days
They catch you unaware
They make your heart race and look to the sky for answers.
Shaking you into existence
They remind you of living and of life.
That you are alive and have a life meant to be lived.

1.

His eyes, they don't sparkle with mischievousness like they used to. It takes him a while to focus, and when he does, you can't quite be sure that he sees you. His memory, it is going. He asks the same things over and over.

"Why are you here?" he asked point blank. "Is this for vacation or is it because I'm old?"

His voice cracked as his self-pity creeped in.

I stuttered, "My job finished so I came."

It wasn't a total lie.

2.

"What is this on my arm? Are these scratches?"

He lifts his mottled brown arm to my face.

"No, Nana. That's your skin."

"Why does it look like this?"

I didn't have the heart to tell him the striations were wrinkles. Instead I said, "Your skin is dry."

3.

I had forgotten, temporarily that we were in Nepal, and that outside there was vibrant life. Indoor, the house is full of the past, a reality full of dementia memories on repeat, all soundtracked to the sound of amplified Nepali puja on amps at the nearby mandar. Sucked into Nana's world is sadness, loneliness on repeat, and isolation brought on by living a life within the 100 steps between his room, the sitting room and balcony. Outside there were majestic the Himalayan mountains, and rolling monsoon clouds, and tropical heat, and filmi music and dirt road traffic, and children playing, laughter and life. Life.

"Which one is he?" I asked, pointing. I look down at the cacophony of children, tugging at each, running around with backpacks and school uniforms. It's recess time at the elementary school next door, and her son is there lost amongst the sweet faces of children.

She doesn't speak English, or Bangla, or Hindi. Only Nepali. But we make do. She shrugs her shoulders, and gives a shy smile, implying he was standing right there but she couldn't find him anymore.

4.

In Kathmandu, it'd be hard to convince me that dementia isn't contagious. I've gone mad. There is not a moment of silence in this town – as the local mandar has been blasting pujas on loudspeakers, and when it's not pujas, it's the Ramayana circa 1980s, blasting through. Loudly. The local Nepali staff says it should be done in another couple days but it's been a week already. Naptime is tainted with maniacal cackles as the some one killed by some demon or something. Sometimes it sounds like Sita is crying.

Nana wanders through the second floor aimlessly asking always what time is it. He wears two watches on his arm. He forgets things quickly, asking things repeatedly, remembering stories as if they happened a month ago, not remembering names of places or things.

He's afraid. He's obsessed with his skin. He thinks we are the crazy ones for needing to scream at him. The monsoon keeps us trapped indoors, and Nana's constant need for company keeps him close by. The constant questions, the wandering aimlessly, his mood swings, all that I can deal with – it's the same old Nana, just more hard of hearing, more blind, less memory, less cantankerous. What I didn't anticipate was the grief. How he replays death. How he sadly he remembers Mom. How he confuses her as my sister.

Or he says she died a month ago. And how he repeats the sad stories, multiple times. I wasn't ready for that. I wasn't ready to feel upset.

5.

"It was you – wasn't it? That it happened to?"

"What? What happened?"

"It was you... it happened during a walk. We were visiting your house. You went and ran to Nani."

"What had happened?"

"You complained that he had hit you with a stick. That you were kicked out of the house."

"How old was I?"

"10 or 12. How old are you now?"

"I'm 34."

Some things your memory just won't let you forget.

6.

"Look under the pillow!"

I lift up the pillow on his bed and underneath it is his watch.

"Why is it here? Are you hiding it?"

"Yes. I'm hiding it from the choor. He'll never find it here."

"There is no choor, Nana. You are surrounded by security guards."

"There is, I know! Or maybe it was a dream."

7.

Under the shade of the green mango tree.

Where the fruit falls before full maturity.

"Is there any use to have these memories?
Tell me?"

Meditation

Alponas spin paisley paths
From the center out
Like dervishes of petals/leaves/lotuses/vines
Spilling white ink from fingertips
Onto dark concrete
Leaving all else
In a thin whirled film
Of rice powder dust
Keep your mind still
Walk your thoughts
Through labyrinths of rangolis

Tanzila "Taz" Ahmed is a poet, writer, activist, politico, organizer, artist, podcaster, strategist, skater, maker, Desi, Muslimah, feminist, lover, fighter, media maker and culture shifter based in Los Angeles.

@TazzyStar

52154198R00048

Made in the USA
Charleston, SC
11 February 2016